Original Beauty: Black Hair in Cyberspace

AYANA A. HAARUUN

MELODYE L. WATSON

DEDICATION

To the black women on YouTube who teach and inspire

CONTENTS

1 INTRODUCTION

> I hope the day will come when women will
> never have to say   I'm going natural' as if its
> something we just purchased. And even maybe
> one day (we'll) be allowed to wear our natural
> hair from childhood into teenage/adulthood so
> that we won't have to google how to take care of
> it. Thanks for all the inspiration and
> encouragement for those of us trying to find our
> way back to where we belong. [sic]

This comment, obtained through observation and content analysis of YouTube natural hair videos, encapsulates the impetus for this study.

The anthropologist Fiana Swain's dissertation on beauty ideals among Black female university students found that of body image, skin and hair, hair affected Black women's self-esteem more than anything else.[i] According to the sociologists Hesse-Biber, Howling, Leavy and Lovejoy, authors of 'Racial Identity and the Development of Body Image Issues among African American Adolescent Girls,' hair is also cited as most exemplary of Black female beauty struggles.[ii] The authors of this study found Black girls' hair represented a struggle for acceptance in both Black and White cultures and is a critical location for issues of self-esteem and body image amongst Black women and girls.

The interconnectedness of hair and Black female beauty is closely linked to issues of race and racism. Although skin colour, body shape and facial features define racial and ethnic affiliation, hair is also an important racial signifier and marker of physiological difference. Hair texture communicates race because tightly coiled short hair denotes strong African ancestry. In a society that favours Eurocentric standards of beauty and puts forth long, straight hair as the hallmark of femininity, a Black woman with tightly coiled short hair could be seen as the antithesis of beauty. As hair can be more easily changed than skin colour, hair has historically represented a popular location for the internalization of racism.

The care and styling of hair that involves straightening represents a paradoxical struggle for Black women. On the one hand, it is a form of Black beautification, while on the other it is often a rejection of Black physical racial attributes.[iii] The fact that hair matters in particular ways for Black women is historically relevant to race and gender relations in Western cultures.[iv] The development of hair hierarchies within Black communities is directly related to colorism, a system of privilege benefitting Blacks and other people of colour with lighter skin and straight hair textures.[v] Within Black hair hierarchies, 'bad' and 'good' hair valuations range from 'tightly coiled' to 'curly' to 'wavy' to 'straight.' Good and bad hair perceptions illustrate Black women's internalization of a long history of White supremacy and their everyday struggles to fit Black hair into White beauty standards.[vi]

Although the socio-political sphere wherein Black women's hair resides is complicated, hairstyling is simply a cultural activity that can be viewed from historical, social, economic and psychological perspectives.[vii] During the early twentieth century, Black beauty culturists, such as Annie Minerva Turnbo Malone and Madame C.J. Walker paved the way for Black hair care entrepreneurs. The term beauty culturist or hair culturist was coined by Madame C.J. Walker and was used to describe the women who were trained to sell and administer Black hair care products and services.[viii] Though they did not challenge the Eurocentric beauty standards of the day, their innovations in Black hair care helped uplift the social standing of Black women

2

by helping them to gain social acceptance in their appearance. During the Great Migration of African Americans from the rural South to Northern cities, Black women were eager to trade in their cornrows, plaits and head coverings for straightened hairstyles to conform to their urban environments. After World War II and throughout the Civil Rights movement, Black women's hair became representative of change within the Black community. It represented the Black community's awareness of its roles as consumers of beauty culture and political agitators. In their fight for racial equality, Black women maintained perfectly coiffed and straightened hair styles that communicated decency and civility. The hairstyles also reflected a willingness to conform to the beauty standards of the dominant White culture in order to gain acceptance. During this period, Black hair care product manufacturers promoted the use of heated straightening combs or hot irons. In the 1960s and 1970s, Black empowerment political and cultural movements inspired the popular Afro hair style. Cultural critic Kobena Mercer asserts the Afro or 'natural' symbolised black people's attempt to construct a positive self-image and collectively link themselves to Africa. [ix] Mercer explains the 1960s slogan 'Black is Beautiful' implied un-straightened afro-textured hair styles were more authentic and in line with Black Power ideology.

The impact of the rejection of Black women's natural physical attributes has fueled the growth of the global, multi-billion dollar Black hair industry. After the 1970s, a new range of black hairstyles emerged. The mass marketing of chemical hair straighteners altered Black beauty culture forever, eventually leading to the curly perm popularly known as the 'Jheri Curl' and boxed hair relaxer kits which dominated the Black hair care product industry during the last two decades of the twenty-first century.[x] Since the 1990s, popular straightened hair styles amongst Black females often include the addition of artificial or human hair extensions. Today, the hair extension industry is the most profitable of the nine billion dollar Black hair business and involves the manufacture of wefts of human hair often sold by women in India, China, Malaysia and Korea.[xi]

On the surface, Black hair beauty culture appears to centre on straight hair as the conduit to Black beauty. However, there has always been resistance to this type of performance of beauty. While some within the Black community attributed racial uplift to the social acceptance and economic mobility gained by Blacks that adhered to Eurocentric beauty standards, others denounced hair straightening as pathological self-hatred and an attempt to emulate White people. Today, more Black women seek to wear their hair in its natural state, not straightened through chemical processes. Unlike the Afro hairstyle trend of the 1960s and 1970s that was inspired by Black empowerment political and cultural movements, the current resurgence in Black women wearing their natural hair is multidimensional. Black women's reasons vary from the financial burden of wearing hair extensions to concerns about the impact of damaging hot irons and hair straightening chemicals on their physical health and mental well-being.

Since the advent of the Internet, online communities have emerged to support, instruct and recognise the growing segment of Black women who desire to wear their natural hair. This study and review of YouTube channels specific to Black women's natural hair was inspired by the researchers' need to care for their own hair. Prior to the proliferation of an Internet natural hair community, there were limited images of black women with natural hair in mass media. Like many women, the researchers were referred by friends to YouTube channels for information about healthy afro-textured hair maintenance and for hair styling ideas. Black women users of YouTube, Twitter, Tumblr, Facebook and other social networking websites have created a virtual pulpit for natural hair that includes social forums, video tutorials, product websites and personal testimonies. Notable periodicals such as The New York Times and The Washington Post have documented the growing trend towards natural hair.[xii] A 2011 report by the market research company Mintel indicated sales of chemical hair straighteners had decreased by 24 percent over five years, and also suggested YouTube as a primary location to attract Black hair product consumers. [xiii] Additionally, websites like YouTube allow users to share information by posting videos and comments, which provides a rich resource for observation and analysis of a virtual support community established in response to a need specific to Black women. Online audiences speak in authentic voices and can yield valuable sociological and ethnographic data.[xiv] Through exploration of the YouTube natural hair community, several themes emerged. Those themes centred on gratitude, praise and identification. Analysis of data gathered from this community provides a reference point for understanding perceptions of beauty, self-esteem and racial pride among Black women.

2 BLACK HAIR

The number of scholarly books, articles or documentaries about Black women's natural hair that also investigates perceptions of beauty is limited. It is important to note that Black women conduct the majority of research on this topic. This point underscores the importance and necessity of Black women creating and further developing knowledge and expertise on subject matters that are relevant within Black communities.

Several histories about Black hair have been written to highlight and explain the impact hair has on Black women. The authors Ayana D. Byrd and Lori L. Tharps explore the social, cultural and economic significance of African-American hair from 1400 to the present in Hair Story: Untangling the Roots of Black Hair in America, which was published in 2002.[xv] Although it is not exhaustive, Byrd and Tharps' chronological review of events in African-American hair history provides a foundation for understanding the complicated relationship Black women have with their hair. The historian Susannah Walker's 2007 book, Style and Status: Selling Beauty to African-American Women 1920-1975, connects the growth and development of Black beauty culture to the Great Migration period when many African-American women left the South to seek better opportunities.[xvi] Walker's history of Black beauty culture makes clear that the standards of beauty influencing Black women were shaped within African-American culture in spite of the influences of the majority culture.[xvii]

Black hair is cited as an historical location for expressions of internalized racism in bell hooks' Outlaw Culture: Resisting Representations, published in 1994.[xviii] hooks discusses the powerful change the Afro hairstyle brought about during the Black Power movements of the 1960s and 1970s in the United States. She also describes the sense of solidarity, pride, and psychological decolonization that resulted from Blacks wearing un-straightened hair during this time. hooks asserts that Black people's later return to hair and skin colour hierarchies happened as a result of a desire to assimilate and obtain social and economic mobility, and she cites the mass media as a major deterrent to many Black people's contemporary reluctance to abandon perceptions of beauty and attractiveness informed by White supremacist notions.[xix] Likewise, the African American Studies scholar Noliwe M. Rooks notes how beauty and culture have politicized African-American women and demonstrates how Western definitions of beauty are often not endorsed by them.[xx] In Hair Raising: Beauty, Culture and African American Women, published in 1996, Rooks investigates the ways in which African-American women developed a niche for themselves within their own families, communities, and national culture through their unique approach to hair and beauty.

As participant observers, the anthropologist Lanita Jacobs-Huey and ethnic studies scholar Ingrid Banks reveal the multi-layered world of African-American women's hair and its many meanings. In From the Kitchen to the Parlor: Language and Becoming in African-American Women's Hair Care, published in 2006, Jacobs-Huey describes her experience as the daughter of a hairstylist as the genesis for her interest in Black hair care and identity. [xxi] Her discussion about Black women's hair is informed through ethnographic discourse analysis that includes cross-racial input about hair as it pertains to African-American women. According to Jacobs-Huey, 'hair is not just hair.'[xxii] This loaded statement implies that for Black women, hair is about race, class, beauty and femininity, and has the ability to express identity. Ingrid Banks' 2000 book, Hair Matters: Beauty, Power, and Black Women's Consciousness affirms that 'hair is a means by which one can understand broader cultural issues.'[xxiii] Banks' analysis of Black women's hair as a measure of identity and power challenges the notion that hair is just a matter of style. Data compiled from Banks ethnographic account reveals that Black women's concern with their hair is tied to their thoughts and feelings about gender politics, racial solidarity, intergenerational difference, and, of course, beauty.[xxiv]

Although the above books have provided historical, social and political contexts for understanding Black hair, critical analysis of how hair - in its unadulterated state - influences all aspects of Black women's lives is greatly needed. Online communities dedicated to Black women with natural hairstyles provide an abundant source of information.

3. BLACK WOMEN ONLINE

As both cultural product and cultural context, the Internet has become a primary location for forming social support groups and virtual communities based upon shared backgrounds or interests.[xxv] Although, global and digital divides are at the root of Black peoples' continued lag in access to and use of the Internet and computing technologies,[xxvi] the number of African-American women attending colleges and universities increased by 400 percent in the last generation.[xxvii] This increase in higher education for African-American women has perhaps resulted in equitable training in information technology with other racial groups,[xxviii] and increased use of computers when compared to African-American men.[xxix]

The women who participate in the YouTube natural hair community (YNHC) can also be understood within the context of Black women's community work, which is linked to the concept of collective identity.[xxx] The sociologist Patricia Hill Collins defines collective identity as an individual's cognitive, moral, and emotional connection with a broader community, category, practices or institutions.[xxxi] Collins' work posits that collective identity is distinct from personal identity, although it may form part of personal identity. Within the African-American community, a syncretic cultural value system from the African

Diaspora serves to foster collective identity and a sense of community. Within our review of YNHC, a Black female virtual 'community' was conceptualized in terms of a social network rather than in terms of physical proximity.[xxxii] According to the information technology specialists Jennifer Preece and Dana Rotman, virtual communities are defined by attributes of shared purpose, participant interaction, user-

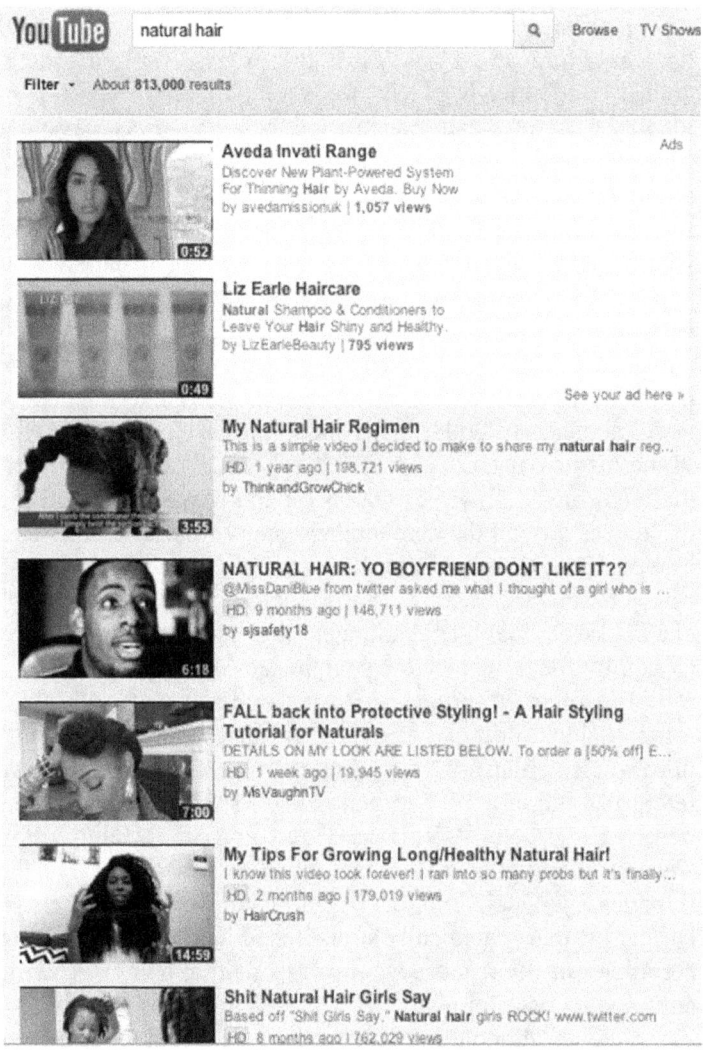

YouTube Search Results for 'Natural Hair'.

generated content, clear boundaries defining the community and unique communal culture.[xxxiii] These qualities are all evident in YNHC.

According to the communications and digital media authors Ananda Mitra and Eric Watts, the process of renegotiating a collective identity is crucial for marginalized groups for whom identity narratives have constructed these groups as the 'other.'[xxxiv] Through online networks marginalized people can identify, articulate and contest identity narratives.[xxxv] Importantly, the Internet can afford modes of resistance and serve as a medium where marginalized individuals can exercise discursive power and resist damaging representations.[xxxvi] Indeed, social networking websites have altered offline traditional power structures and empowered marginal entities to challenge dominate voices.[xxxvii]

Launched in 2005, YouTube is the fastest growing website in the history of the web.[xxxviii] YouTube has helped redistribute the mass media power of television and played a critical role in discourses around the democratization of cultural production.[xxxix] The 'viral' and social nature of YouTube provides a free space for continuous video and text-based interactions,[xl] a characteristic that has facilitated the development of YNHC. Certainly, Black women have embraced YouTube.

The Internet and access to mass media, notes the feminist artist Faith Wilding, provide women and girls with an unparalleled platform to promote their 'voices, languages, interests, and art.'[xli] The journalism student Tricia Scruggs' paper 'I Am Not My Hair: How YouTube Culture Powers Change' highlights how Black women embraced YouTube's 'broadcast yourself' motto, began posting videos of themselves cutting off their chemically straightened hair and produced video chronicles of their 'journeys' towards natural hair.[xlii] The digital culture theorist Pramod Nayer refers to these types of video blogs as 'technologies of self-representation for public consumption.'[xliii] In Watching YouTube: Extraordinary Videos by Ordinary People, published in 2010, the communications scholar Michael Strangelove claims that YouTube offers a space for a more radical, complex and distinct Black female voice.[xliv] 'Some of the most extraordinary videos on YouTube are produced by Black women who are struggling to define themselves,' Strangelove writes.[xlv] On YouTube, Black female video bloggers often broadcast from their private spaces and discuss Black cultural and identity politics. [xlvi] In subjective voices, they narrate and communicate autobiographical cultural experiences and express ideas they find personally relevant.[xlvii] In YNHC, Black women assert control over technology, self-representation and interaction with spectators.[xlviii]

Female video bloggers' emphasis on pursuing female empowerment through personal concerns could be read as an expression of cyberfeminist practice.[xlix] Cyberfeminist theorists resist strict definitions of cyberfeminism and aspire to a decentered and participatory practice relevant to women in the information age.[l] One cyberfeminist practitioner suggested cyberfeminism aims to 'examine the relationships between women and technology; critique equality in cyberspace; examine relationships between bodies and technology; examine technology by engaging with it; disrupt the perception of technology as 'toys for boys;' seek to induce change from within; and playfully, subtly or directly address feminist issues.'[li] Cyberfeminist collectives have been smaller than established feminist groups and more concerned with the individual subjective expression of ideas rather than articulating canonized feminist thought.[lii] Diverse forms of female empowerment seem the best focus of cyberfeminism.

The practices of Black women within YNHC appear aligned with aspects of the cyberfeminist movement. Through media production technology and the Internet, Black women and girls have transformed and expanded traditional beauty shop dialogues in ways that disrupt not only racial but gender stereotypes. In authentic voices, they share with other women their experiences as mothers, students, workers, artists, spiritualists and entrepreneurs. They discuss mastering various technologies and offer critiques of patriarchy, White beauty standards and racism, while promoting collaborative women's economic empowerment. In YNHC, women succeed at creating affirmative and complex images of Black women that break popular mediated representations of both Blackness and femininity.

There is a wealth of feminist and gender scholarship that considers how the 'gaze,' a form of power-laden staring, produces and enforces gendered positions. Traditional feminist analysis presumes that the mass media is part of an objectifying process that provides spectators the opportunity to look at and have power over women's bodies. In 'Too Close To See: Men, Women, and Webcams,' Internet studies scholar Michele White suggests that female webcam operators express resistant modes of address and do not fully produce images for the male gaze, but rather for themselves. In YNHC, many female video bloggers exhibit themselves 'undone' and share their beautification processes with their audiences. Such access to Black women's authentic physical attributes forces spectators to confront unaltered Black female bodies. Since the primary spectators of YouTube natural hair videos are Black women and girls, the notion of a feminine 'gaze' and voyeurism as they relate to women looking at other women takes form. According to White, this type of spectatorship can result in desire, fascination and personal empowerment.[liii]

4. THE YOUTUBE NATURAL HAIR COMMUNITY

This study employed a survey and applied an online ethnography approach called netnography.[liv] Netnography is a quantitative research methodology designed specifically for participatory or observational study of online networks and communities.[lv] Eleven YouTube videos were examined as well as 5226 public comments posts. Video selection was based upon four criteria: designation within YouTube's 'Howto & Style' category;[lvi] 50,000 or more views, display of data tags for 'natural' and 'hair,' and diversity of video content. Data collection utilized Tams Analyzer (TA), computer software published by May Day Softworks. All comments posted on selected YouTube web pages were saved as Portable Document Format (PDF) files and imported into the software. While we do not display them here for privacy's sake, we maintained hyperlinks to YouTube videos, which allowed easy access to videos and video channel webpages. Using an open coding procedure, codes were created and assigned to comment posts. Posts with data relevant in more than one category resulted in overlapping codes.[lvii] Data categorization focused on defining the YouTube natural hair culture, the politics of Black hair, viewer identification with video performers and expressions of support, gratitude, and praise. One hundred and eighty-five responses from a web-based survey were analysed to assess YNHC

15

Map of YNHC Participant Ethnic Identification and Geographic Location.

members' knowledge and beliefs about natural-haired Black women.

The 'Community' category for data analyses was established to formulate a sense of the YouTube natural hair culture, its participants and its boundaries. Ninety-nine percent of participants in YNHC identified as being of African descent and female. Data also suggested community participants of various ethnicities living around the world. YouTube analytics reported top audience locations for videos in this study were from the United States, Canada, the United Kingdom and several Caribbean nations.[lviii] We reviewed YouTube Video Statistics which include top audience demographics and location for each video in this study. In comments, female participants alluded to national and ethnic identification such as Moroccan, Ghanaian, Ethiopian, Nigerian, Eritrean, Cameroonian, Trinidadian, Guyanese, Bahamian, Jamaican, Afro-Brazilian and Afro-French descent. Other participants and video makers revealed they lived in Europe, Canada, the United Kingdom, France, South Africa, Ghana, Japan, Barbados, Germany or Holland. Their comments were posted in English, French or Spanish. The multinational participation of women within YHNC confirms Black hair as an identifying racial characteristic important enough to serve as a binding force for building a social network and anchoring a digital Diaspora (Map 1).

YNHC communication patterns were complex and highly interactive. Messages were exchanged via public post, private video channel inbox and video reply. Community membership was denoted through direct references to YNHC and through terms like 'us,' 'we,' 'ladies,' and 'subbie' (subscriber). Posts also expressed a strong sense of 'sisterhood' within the community. Many participants used endearment terms such as 'girl,' 'sister,' 'princess,' or 'doll' to address one another.

The use of unique terminology is a defining cultural element of cyber cultures.[lix] Participants in YNHC often use beauty affirming pseudonyms and channel names such as: 'Love Your Curls', 'Mahogany Curls' or 'Coloured Beautiful.' Participants also create and employ original terms and acronyms to reference Black hair and online natural hair culture including 'twa' (teenie weenie Afro), 'BC' (big chop; cutting off chemically straightened hair), 'twist out' (a popular natural hairstyle), 'transitioning' (the process of growing natural hair with existing chemically straightened hair), and 'hair anniversary' (annual date following cutting chemically straightened-hair.)

Data also suggests the YNHC community is multigenerational. YouTube.com analytics, which aggregates data on usage, reported top demographics for videos in this study were females between the ages of eighteen and forty-four.[lx] However, comments such as the following imply that girls as young as eleven are involved in the community: 'Hi im simbahsuccessful26 but my real name is EGYPT, i am 12 yrs old and im now transitioning without the big chop and im soooooo super, extremly, happy about going back to my natural hair:).' [sic]

This data points to the fact that Black women's participation within beauty culture begins in childhood, as does their struggle with their hair. For Black girls, hair hierarchies and the social impediments of un-straightened afro-textured hair are internalized early. The following post illustrates a girl's fear of wearing her natural hair, and the social challenges she faces:

> i want to go natural but im scared of chopping all my hair off. :(i have no support from my family members they all say that its ugly and nappy is not right. but i want to see what MY NATURAL HAIR can do and how i look with it. i want to be naturally beautiful :(but i have no support and im still in high school__ so ill get BASHED for going to school with "natural hair"... people are so mean [sic]

Through hairstyling, Black mothers play critical roles in transmitting positive or negative values about Black hair and beauty. In a discussion on Nikkimae 2003's YouTube page, participants shared stories of having chemical straighteners applied to their hair when they were as young as three years old and also confided the difficulties of gaining their mother's acceptance of their natural hair. The following post is indicative of the support YNHC adult participants provide to girls seeking to wear their natural hair:

> My mom nearly had a heart attack when I wanted to go natural. Even though it has been about 2 years she still has negative things to say. You have to do it for you no one else. Recognize it may be a generational thing because older Black people were conditioned to view their natural hair as ugly. Explain why you want to go natural and educate yourself and go for it. a great style for transitioning are roller sets with perm or flexirods, and braids outs. I say go for it.=) [sic]

In NaturallyNew's 'Transition from Relaxed to Natural Hair 2 Years Anniversary! No Big Chop' video, a mother narrates a video slideshow of photographs of her daughter's hairstyles and hair grooming. This video is exemplary of the many mothers who participate in YNHC or who come to the community seeking information on caring for their daughters' hair. Participants expressed that this video served as motivation to continue growing their hair without chemical straighteners.

In online dialogues, discussions often reproduce existing racism and racial stereotypes found within offline societies.lxi Although less than 2 percent of the total posts analyzed in this study implied negative sentiments towards the video performer's beauty or hair, those few denigrating sentiments led to heated exchanges that were often addressed and rebutted by participants. The only YouTube Featured Video included in this study wasTaren916's 'The Huetiful Steamer Review.' Featured Videos functions as YouTube video advertisements and are presented to a larger audience. Taren916's Featured Video received over 460,000 views and almost 1500 comments.lxii Comments posted in response to this video indicated male spectatorship as well as disapproval of the video performer, Black natural hair, and Black women's attractiveness. The following dialogue is an example of a discussion about Black beauty ignited on Tarin916's featured video page: (Some comments were deleted by Tarin 916.)

> im not usually that attracted to Black people but ive got_ to say, she is BEAUTIFUL.
> -jonknutton

> Oh Yeah. Just saw your photo........ No comment... Wait. Never-mind... I'm just going to say it.... You are ugly! Honest truth. Your skin color has nothing to do with it. You're just not attractive. No joke.!
> -ebonyhatcber in reply to jonknutton

> I dont have a photo?! And just to clarify im not being racist.   My personal preference doesn't make me racist. I have nothing   against Black people im just not USUALLY attracted to them. However this woman is next level.

19

-jonknutton in reply to ebonyhatcber

Nothing wrong with personal preference. I prefer large   penises. So I tend to date Black guys. I mean, there! is   nothing wrong with the White man small penis, I just prefer a large one.:) So you're right. Sorry for jumping to conclusions:)
-ebonyhatcber in reply to jonknutton

Racism works both! ways you know. The only difference is we're proud of who we are (generally speaking). If you were too you wouldn't be offended every time someone says the word Black.
-jonknutton in reply to ebonyhatcber

You could've simply said that she is beautiful, which she is. You say that you're statement wasn't an attempt to degrade anyone but it does. You didn't even say black women, you said people encompassing both genders. So next time when you want to compliment someone just compliment, don't insult a whole race of people to do it, unless of course you are   racist which! is your right then be man enough to have the courage of your convictions.
-TheNuyorker in reply to jonknutton [sic]

Respondents to jonknutton are an example of cyber community 'police.' These participants help establish and maintain the social norms of cyber communities.[lxiii] This kind of direct refutation serves as an expression of the collective thought and subversive agenda of YNHC which is to promote Black hair in its natural state as beautiful, and in turn promotes Black

20

women as beautiful.

Despite dialogues about race, YNHC was generally racially and ethnically inclusive. In YNHC women who identified as non-Black or biracial served as participants and video bloggers. Nonetheless, video performers' actual hair texture served as an important racial identifier and a critical aspect of information sharing and the viewer identification process. Participants expressed happiness in accessing images of women with similar hair texture and inquired about the racial identity of video performers with longer hair or loosely-coiled hair textures. These inquiries into the video performers' race and ethnicity seemed a means for discerning whether the participant could attain the video performer's hairstyle. Taren 916's featured video page contained discriminatory comments made in regards to her biracial identity and her loosely coiled hair texture. Participants expressed that her wavy hair provided an unachievable reference for other Black women.

5 SUPPORT

Cyberfeminist theorists hypothesize that women and girls often form virtual kinships focused on support.[lxiv] Since YNHC functions like other Internet support groups, researchers developed a 'support' category for classifying data. Cutrona and Suhr's 'Social Support Behaviour Codes' (SSBC), a well-known inventory tool for categorizing social support behaviours was employed in this study.[lxv] SSBC categorizes social support behaviours by information supports, tangible assistance, esteem support, network support, and emotional support.[lxvi] All SSBC categories of social support were identified in posts and video transcriptions of YouTube natural hair videos.

Diagram 1 indicates 'praise' and represents the highest amount of data in the support category. Praise was considered as a form of esteem support. Expressions of praise often referenced aspects of a video performer's hair, beauty, or personality. For example: Girl your hair is the BOMB! And you're beautiful! Too.' [sic]

Video performers often responded to participant praise with expressions of gratitude. Perhaps the self-concept of video performers was also positively impacted by numerous expressions of praise for their beauty, hair and personality.

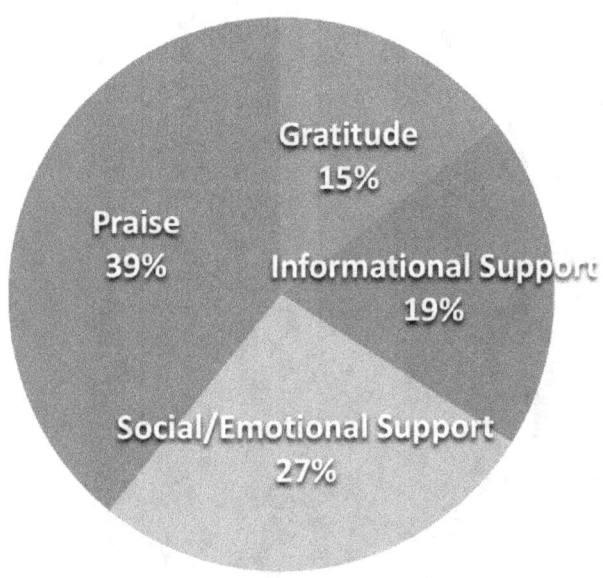

Diagram 1. Percentage of Support-Related Comments by Category

Furthermore, participants expressed praise of their own hair and validated Black beauty and hair. These posts embody self-acceptance, racial pride and naturally achievable beauty ideals, all of which perhaps motivate Black women to embrace their natural hair. The following post is an example of praise for Black hair: 'I always wondered what it would be like if every Black woman in the world embraced her natural hair? I think the whole world would dramatically change its perception of Black hair. Because we are the only people with our hair, i think we would become the envy of the entire world :P.' [sic]

Moreover, all YNHC videos included in this study show women grooming their own hair rather than visiting a beauty salon. This practice is a defining feature of the online natural hair world, which contrasts with the prevailing, mainstream U.S.

Images from 'Flaxseed/Linseed Gel Homemade,' Video. Courtesy of 1Ballerina.

Images from 'Short Natural Hair: How I Refresh My Wash n Go (The In-Between Stage)' Video. Courtesy of MahoganyCurls.

Black beauty culture where an average woman can spend thousands of dollars annually on beauty shop visits. Also, many of the products that video performers exhibit and reference are inexpensive and made of natural ingredients. For example, 1Ballerina's 'Flaxseed/Linseed Gel Homemade' video, is a tutorial showing the manufacture of an inexpensive hair gel made from raw flaxseed and linseed. The do-it-yourself practices of YNHC encourage commerce amongst women and a prudent approach to beautification processes.

Demonstrations of social or emotional support within YNHC occurred in discussions about personal hair experiences and the social, emotional and psychological challenges of wearing afro-textured hair. When participants expressed frustration, fear, or a need for encouragement, others responded with encouraging words or practical advice. Posts also revealed the frustration participants felt about their hair. For example: 'lol angry is such a good word to describe my hair'[lxvii] was posted by a follower in response to another follower who described her frustration with her 'angry' and 'frizzy' hair.

Nikkimae 2003's 'Natural Hair Lessons Learned Part 1' shows the video blogger with a very large Afro hairstyle. In a confessional manner, Nikkiemae 2003 addresses her audience and then explains the discomfort and challenges she endured growing out her chemically-relaxed hair.

> So I started to get really discouraged you guys. It was a rough time for me. My self esteem started to go down tremendously. I just remember waking up in the morning and looking at my head and wanting to cry because it just looked so horrible....I was really enjoying seeing what my natural texture looked like. I hadn't seen my natural hair since I was like six. I mean, I started getting relaxers when I was six, so I had no idea what to expect with that. [sic]

Numerous participants related to NikkieMae 2003 story of being completely unaware of how their natural hair actually looked and of being initially ignorant about how to care for it.

Later in her video, Nikkimae 2003 expresses appreciation for the support she received from the online natural hair community and says she was inspired to 'go natural' after seeing other women on a popular blog site cutting off their chemically straightened hair:

> I remember one of the first sites she showed me was CurlyNikki.com, and when I saw that site I was motivated through the roof. She had this series going on where she was looking at people who were doing the big chops. And I couldn't believe how brave all this women were for just cutting off their hair and going natural. I was like wow people do this? And that was really encouraging to me and that started me on the route of looking at youtube videos and seeing how people were transitioning, and learning about transitioning styles. I was like wow, I can do this. If everyone here can do it, I can do it too. [sic]

Participants responded to NikkieMae 2003's video with comments regarding their own struggles with self-esteem and the assistance YNHC provides, with posts like the following: 'Thank you so so very much for continuing to do these videos. You were one of my inspirations for going natural. Along with the other natural woman on YouTube my self-confidence, the way people see me and the way I see myself have all changed in a positive way.' [sic]

Frequent expressions of gratitude were indicative of the value participants had for receiving information, support, and accessing images of women with afro-textured hair. Participants noted the 'journey' to appreciating and wearing their natural hair was an all-encompassing, physical, psychological and even spiritual endeavour. For some, wearing natural hair meant looking 'the way God intended.'

6 VIEWER IDENTIFICATION

YouTube's function as a user-generated alternative to broadcast television and film was examined in this study. Theories of spectator identification with on-screen characters were identified in relation to the impact of viewer identification with amateur video performers. The telecommunications author Peter Van Beneden asserts identification with on-screen characters includes devotion and adoration, desire to become more like the film actor, and aspiration toward the actor's personality, behaviour and confidence.[lxviii] Van Beneden forwards the notion that audiences are not passive recipients of media messages but instead seek out particular media content because they are motivated by specific goals, needs, desires and/or preferences.[lxix] Diagram 2 highlights the viewer identification by category.

Studies of viewer attachment to media characters show viewers are more attracted to characters and personalities whom they perceive as similar to themselves. This perception of similarity often results in audiences viewing media characters as 'role models' whom they aspire to be like.[lxx] In this study, posts in which participants articulate personal resemblance with video performers were often complementary both to the video performer and the commenter. For example: 'Our hair is exactly the same and I love yours as well as mine!!!' [sic]

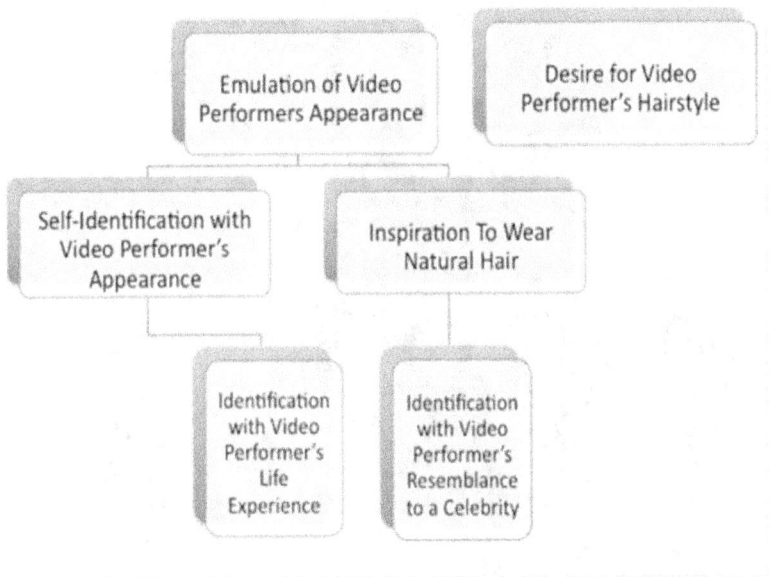

Diagram 2. Viewer Identification Comments by Category

According to Michele White, when compared to cinematic viewing, computer on-screen viewing can create an even more partial sense of familiarity and increase the spectators' sense of closeness to the video performer.[lxxi] By directly addressing audiences, video performers in YNHC perhaps increase viewers' sense of familiarity and intimacy. Data shows viewers made hyper-detailed observations of video content and personally identified with video performers' appearance, hair, personality, location, experience or perceived environment. Participants were 'fans' of video performers[lxxii] whom they viewed as inspiring role models with the status of micro-celebrities.[lxxiii]

Fusion of Cultures' 14 minute video '6 Months Natural -

Images from Fusion of Cultures (Laila Jean), '6 Months Natural Single Strand Knots Shea Butter Winners Length Check,' Video. Courtesy of Fusion of Cultures.

Single Strand Knots -Shea Butter Winners -Length Check,' exhibits a more performative style of video blogging. Her channel information section indicates her age as 23, location as the United Kingdom and 'big chop date' as July 7, 2011. In the video included in this study, Fusion of Cultures appears well-dressed, wears makeup and has shoulder length styled hair. In a British accent and with animated hand gestures, she sends New Year's well wishes to her audience and apologizes for her absence. She talks about her holiday, family and Ghanaian heritage. As the video progresses, she answers frequently asked questions about her hair maintenance routine.

Judging from her 38,717 subscribers, numerous complimentary posts, and 'giveaway' participation, Fusion of Cultures has reached the status of 'micro-celebrity.' Many participants indicated they would emulate hairstyles or use tips shown in her videos, or shared in other participant comments. With long afro-textured hair Fusion of Cultures provided a practical reference for participants to desire, emulate or aspire to. The desire to have longer natural hair like Fusion of Cultures was the most commonly expressed of all posts included in this study. Consider the following representative post: '**DROOLS OVER COMPUTER KEYBOARD** Girl, ILOOOOVE everything about your hair!! My goal is to get to your length by end of this year, God-willing :).' [sic]

The term 'parasocial relationship' has been used to describe the bond viewers develop with screen characters over time. Audiences can develop emotional attachments with mediated representations and feel as if they know video performers personally.[lxxiv] Six percent of participants within YNHC revealed that they had visited a video performer's channel more than once, while other described themselves as 'followers' or 'subscribers.' All video channels included in this study contained multiple videos post over multi-year spans. Posts indicate viewers often followed the performer's hair growth progress and channel updates over many years. The results of this study indicate viewers of YouTube natural hair videos are heavily influenced in ways similar to television and film mediums. Data indicates viewers sought out women with similar hair textures, hair lengths and hairstyles, and used video blogs for inspirational references. Perceived self-resemblance to video performers' appearance, personality or life experience also played a key role in impacting viewers' sense of closeness with video performer, and positively reinforced participants' self-concept and self-perceptions of beauty.

7 SURVEY

To further assess how members of YNHC feel about natural hair, a brief survey was administered. 1Ballerina, a YouTube blogger, posted a link to the survey on her channel, along with a video requesting her followers to complete the Original Beauty Survey on Black Women and Natural Hair. We asked 1Ballerina to post the survey. Approximately 185 respondents completed the survey, which consisted of the following ten statements to which respondents stated they either agreed or disagreed. In some instances, respondents neither agreed nor disagreed.

- I like the way my natural hair looks.

- Wearing my hair natural makes me feel good.

- Wearing my hair natural is healthy.

- Natural hair on Black women looks attractive.

- I look attractive when I wear my hair natural.

- I like to see Black women wear natural hairstyles.

- Black women that wear their hair natural have racial pride.

- Black women's hairstyle choices reflect their political and cultural views.

- I have visited YouTube to learn about caring for and styling natural hair.

- YouTube blogger channels and other online resources provide support for Black women to wear natural hairstyles.

Survey results suggest that respondents overwhelmingly agreed with positive statements about Black women wearing their hair natural. Key findings from the survey, listed below, reinforce the analysis of data and demonstrate that Black women with natural hair are affirmed and supported by their participation in YNHC. Statements aimed at assessing opinions about Black natural hair as attractive, likeable and healthy infer that self-esteem is positively affected for Black women.

- Of the respondents, 92 percent indicated they liked the way their natural hair looks.

- Of the respondents, 95 percent indicated wearing their hair natural made them feel good.

- Nearly 99 percent of respondents affirmed wearing hair natural is healthy.

- Of the respondents, 98 percent agreed natural hair looks attractive on Black women.

- Only 8 percent of respondents stated that they did not like to see Black women wear natural hairstyles.

- Of the respondents, 90 percent disagreed that Black women's hairstyles communicated cultural or political views.

- More than half (60 percent) of respondents indicated

Black women with natural hair are expressing racial pride.

8 CONCLUSION

The findings of this study barely scratch the surface of the types of information that can be gleaned from critical investigation of the YouTube natural hair community as it relates to Black women, beauty and the medium of social networking sites as a conduit for expression. Technology has brought about a means for Black women in the African Diaspora to connect in ways not possible previously. As more Black women seek out information about natural hair care, the online communities that exist to support them will expand. This expansion will likely reinforce acceptance of natural hair as beautiful and the norm, and therefore increase self-esteem and racial pride for Black women.

The implications of this research are broad with the potential to inform various interests. Mainstream media, hair care and beauty product manufacturers and hair stylists are just a few of the many interests that would benefit from a better understanding of this unique online community. Those interested in improving the behavioural health outcomes for Black women have a strong impetus for examining these online communities as a source of information for developing resources.

There are limitations to this study. The researchers acknowledge the need for expansion of the survey to include online focus groups that would further knowledge development on this community. The researchers also acknowledge comparable online videos of Black women with chemically straightened hairstyles and hair extensions exist and are deserving of critical inquiry to make inferences about perceptions of beauty, self-esteem and racial pride for a broad range of Black women.

ABOUT THE AUTHORS

Ayana Haaruun, serves as Chair and Professor of Media Communications at Kennedy-King College in Chicago, IL, USA. Her research explores cyber cultures, women and technology and black popular culture.

Melodye Watson, is a behavior therapist and social worker. She studies the intersectionality of race, gender and religion.

ii Fiana O. Swain, 'Negotiating Beauty Ideals: Perceptions of Beauty among Black Female University Students' (MA thesis. Georgia State University, 2012).

ii Sharlene Nagy Hesse-Biber et al., 'Racial Identity and the Development of Body Image Issues Among African American Adolescent Girls,' The Qualitative Report 9 no. 1 (March 2004): 67-69.

iii Ibid.

NOTES

iv Susannah Walker, Style and Status: Selling Beauty to African American Women 1920-1975 (Lexington: University of Kentucky Press, 2007).

v Ibid.

vi Cynthia Robinson, 'Hair as Race: Why 'Good Hair' May be Bad for Black Women,' Howard Journal of Communications 22, no. 4 (November 2011): 360

vii Kobena Mercer, Welcome to the Jungle (New York: Routledge, 1994), 97.

viii Walker, Style and Status, 42.

ix Ibid.

x Ibid.

xi 'Chris Rock on the Billion Dollar Black "Good Hair" Industry,' Oprah.com, last modified 4 November 2009, viewed 1 November 2012,

http://www.cnn.com/2009/LIVING/homestyle/11/04/o.chris.rock.good.hair/index.html.

xiiNina Saro-Wiwa. 'Black Women's Transition to Natural Hair,' The New York Times, 1 June 2012, viewed 11 June 2012, http://www.nytimes.com/2012/06/01/opinion/Black-women-and-natural-hair.html?_r=0.

Danielle Douglas. 'Roots and Revenue: The Popularity of Natural Hairstyles is Lucrative for Local Salons,' The Washington Post, 7 March 2012, viewed 21 March, 2012,

http://www.washingtonpost.com/business/capitalbusiness/roots-and-revenue-the-popularity-of-natural-hairstyles-is-lucrative-for-local-salons/2012/03/07/gIQAOkgL5R_story.html.

xiii Mintel Report Database MRd 2011,'Black Hair Care -United States-August 2011,' Mintel.com, viewed on 20 March 2012, http://www.oyxgen.mintel.com, 12.

xiv Jean Burgess and Joshua Green, YouTube: Online Video and Participatory Culture (Cambridge: Polity Press, 2009), 22.

xv Ayana Byrd and Lori Tharps, Hair Story: Untangling the Roots of Black Hair in America (New York: Macmillan, 2002).

xvi Walker, Style and Status, 33.

xvii Ibid.

xviii bell hooks, Outlaw Culture: Resisting Representations (New York: Routledge, 1994), 204-213.

xix Ibid.

xx Noliwe M. Rooks, Hair Raising: Beauty, Culture and African American Women (London and New Brunswick: Rutgers University Press, 1996).

xxi Lanita Jacobs-Huey, From the Kitchen to the Parlor: Language and African American Women's Hair Care (Oxford: Oxford University Press, 2006).

xxii Ibid.

xxiii Ingrid Banks, Hair Matters: Beauty, Power and Black Women's Consciousness (New York: NY Press, 2000).

xxiv Ibid.

xxv Liav Sade-Beck. 'Internet Ethnography: Online and Offline,' International Journal of Qualitative Methods 3, no. 2 (2004): 46-47.

xxvi Kayla D. Hales and Lynette Kvasny, 'Identity (Re)evaluation in Cyberspace' (paper presented at the International Conference on ICT for Africa 2010, Yaoundé, Cameroon, March 25-28, 2010, viewed 28 July 2012, http://faculty.ist.psu.edu/lkvasny/KvasnyHales-DigitalDivideChapter_Revised_.pdf. In this paper, the authors assert the 'digital divide' was initially 'defined as a lack of physical access to computing devices necessary to obtain Internet access' and 'concerns related to disparities in information literacy and skills necessary to function proficiently on the Internet.' 'Global divide' was defined as the 'separation between wired countries from those with little access to the network.'

xxvii Michelle Wright, 'Finding a Place in Cyberspace: Black Women, Technology, and Identity,' Frontiers: A Journal of Women Studies 26, no. 1 (2005): 48-59.

xxviii Ibid.

xxixMary Frank Fox, Deborah G. Johnson and Sue V. Rosser, Women, Gender and Technology (Champaign-Urbana: University of Illinois Press, 2006), 103.

xxx YouTube Natural Hair Community (YNHC) is a term coined by the authors to describe girls and women who post videos about afro-textured natural hair or participate in dialogues on YouTube webpages focused on natural hair.

xxxi Patricia Hill Collins, From Black Power to Hip-Hop: Racism, Nationalism and Feminism (Philadelphia: Temple University Press, 2006).

xxxii Mark A. Smith and Peter Kollock, eds., Communities in Cyberspace (London: Routledge, 1999), 17.

xxxiii Preece and Rotman, 'The "WeTube" in YouTube: Creating an Online Community Through Video Sharing,' 320.

xxxiv Ananda Mitra and Eric Watts, 'Theorizing Cyberspace: the Idea of Voice Applied to the Internet Discourse,' New Media and Society 4, no. 4 (2002): 485.

xxxv Hales and Kvasny, 'The African Diaspora, Black Identity and the Evolving Discourse of the Digital Divide,' 3.

xxxvi Mitra and Watts, 'Theorizing Cyberspace: the Idea of Voice Applied to the Internet Discourse,' 486.

xxxvii Ibid.

xxxviii Pelle Snickars and Patrick Vondreau, The YouTube Reader (Stockholm: National Library of Sweden, 2009), 11.

xxxix Burgess and Green, YouTube: Online Video and Participatory Culture, 22.

xl Jennifer Preece and Dana Rotman, 'The 'WeTube' in YouTube: Creating an Online Community Through Video Sharing,' International Journal of Web Based Communities 6, no. 3 (2010), 322.

xli Faith Wilding, 'Where is the Feminism in Cyber Feminism,' N.paradoxa International Feminist Art Journal 2 (1998), ktpress.co.uk, viewed 1 November 2012, http://www.ktpress.co.uk/pdf/vol2_npara_6_13_Wilding.pdf.

xlii Tricia Scruggs, 'I Am Not My Hair: How YouTube Culture Powers Change,' viralmedia.pbworks.com, viewed 13 November 2012, http://viralmedia.pbworks.com/w/file/fetch/53605654/I%20Am%20 Not%20My%20Hair-%20EMAC%206372.pdf.

xliii Pramod K. Nayer, An Introduction to New Media and Cybercultures (West Sussex: Wiley-Blackwell, 2010), 94.

xliv Michael Strangelove, Watching YouTube: Extraordinary Videos by Ordinary People (Toronto: University of Toronto Press, 2010).

xlv Ibid.

xlvi Michele White, 'Too Close To See: Men, Women, and Webcams,' New Media & Society 5, no. 1 (2003): 11.

xlvii Burgess and Green, YouTube: Online Video and Participatory Culture, 48.

xlviii Nayer, An Introduction to New Media and Cybercultures, 94.

xlix Kristine Blair, Radhika Gajjala, and Christine Tulley, eds., Webbing Cyberfeminist Practice: Communities, Pedagogies, and Social Action (New York: Hampton Press: 2009).

l Wilding, 'Where is the Feminism in Cyber Feminism.'

li sajbrfem, 'Cyberfeminism 101,' slideshare.net, viewed on 11 November 2012, http://www.slideshare.net/sajbrfem/cyberfeminism-101.

lii Ibid.

liii White, 'Too Close To See: Men, Women, and Webcams,' 8, 21.

liv Robert V. Kozinets, Netnography: Doing Ethnographic Research Online (London: Sage Publications, 2010).

lv Ibid.

lvi 'Category,' viewed 16 October 2012, www.youtube.com. Videos post on YouTube can be categorized under the 'Browse' tab.

lvii Galit Nimrod, 'Online Communities as A Resource in Older Adults' Tourism,' The Journal of Community Informatics 8, no. 1 (2012): 4.

lviii http://www.youtube.com/yt/advertise/youtubeanalytics.html,viewed on 15 June 2012. YouTube video channels include a statistics section that describes top audience demographics and location. This data is inclusive of age and gender. YouTube analytics is a self - service tool that gives detailed statistics on videos and viewers for advertising purposes.

lix Christine Hine, Virtual Ethnography (London: Sage Publications, 2000).

lx

http://www.youtube.com/yt/advertise/youtubeanalytics.html,viewed on 15 June 2012. YouTube video channels include a statistics section that describes top audience demographics and location. This data is inclusive of age and gender. YouTube analytics is a self-service tool that gives detailed statistics on videos and viewers for advertising purposes.

lxiHales and Kvasny, 'The African Diaspora, Black Identity and the Evolving Discourse of the Digital Divide,' 5.

lxii'Featured Videos,' Youtube.com, last modified 16 October 2012, viewed on 16 October 12,

http://support.google.com/youtube/bin/answer.py?hl=en&answer=1 43421. Featured videos come from YouTube's commercial partners, 'but may also include select user videos that are currently popular or that have previously showcased in spotlight videos.

lxiii Burgess and Green, YouTube: Online Video and Participatory Culture, 96.

lxiv Blair, Gajjala and Tulley, Webbing Cyberfeminist Practice.

lxv Qian and Mao, 'A Content Analysis of Online Social Support Behaviors of Overseas Chinese Prenatal and Postnatal Women,'

China Media Report Overseas, 2010, viewed 21 May 2012, http://www.thefreelibrary.com/A+content+analysis+of+online+soci al+support+behaviors+of+overseas...-a0242509930. Cutrona and Suhr's Social Support Behavior Codes categorize 23 social behaviors into five categories: information supports, tangible assistance, esteem support, network support, and emotional support.

lxvi Ibid.

lxvii MissDarcei, [n.d.], comment on Mahogany Curls, 'Short Natural Hair: How I Refresh My Wash n Go (The In-Between Stage),' 8 March 2012, YouTube.com, viewed 7June 2012 (2:58 p.m.), http://www.youtube.com/all_comments?v=1PT9ohmmWPE.

lxviii Peter van Beneden, 'Viewer 'Identification' with Characters in Television and Film Fiction,' 11 November 2008, www.aber.ac.uk, viewed on 22 May 2012, http://www.aber.ac.uk/media/Students/pjv9801.html.

lxix 'Attachment to Media Characters: Theoretical Approaches, Components of Attraction, Parasocial Attachment, Audience Characteristics that Affect Parasocial Attachment, encyclopedia.jrank.org, viewed 1 November, 2012, http://encyclopedia.jrank.org/articles/pages/6428/Attachment-to-Media-Characters.html#ixzz2D9lZM35d.

lxx Ibid.

lxxi White, The Body and the Screen, 58.

lxxii Burgess and Green, YouTube, 12.

lxxiii Theresa M. Senft, Camgirls: Celebrity & Community in the Age of Social Networks (New York: Peter Lang Publishing, 2008),

25. 'Micro-celebrity' was described as 'a popular cultural phenomenon and style of online performance people 'amping up' their popularity over the web using videos, blogs, and social networking sites.'

lxxiv Ibid.

REFERENCES

'Attachment to Media Characters: Theoretical Approaches, Components of Attraction, Parasocial Attachment, Audience Characteristics that Affect Parasocial Attachment.' encyclopedia.jrank.org. Viewed 1 November, 2012. http://encyclopedia.jrank.org/articles/pages/6428/Attachment-to-Media-Characters.html#ixzz2D9lZM35d.

Banks, Ingrid. Hair Matters: Beauty, Power and Black Women's Consciousness. New York: NYU Press, 2000.

Blair, Kristine, Radhika Gajjala, and Christine Tulley, eds. Webbing Cyberfeminist Practice: Communities, Pedagogies, and Social Action. New York: Hampton Press, 2009.

Burgess, Jean and Joshua Green. YouTube: Online Video and Participatory Culture. Cambridge: Polity Press, 2001.

Byrd, Ayana and Lori Tharps. Hair Story: Untangling the Roots of Black Hair in America. New York: Macmillan, 2002.

'Chris Rock on the Billion Dollar Black 'Good Hair' Industry,' Oprah.com, last modified 4 November 2009. Viewed 1 November 2012. http://www.cnn.com/2009/LIVING/homestyle/11/04/o.chris.rock.good.hair/index.html.

Collins, Patricia Hill. From Black Power to Hip-Hop: Racism, Nationalism and Feminism. Philadelphia: Temple University Press, 2006.

'Cyberfeminism 101.' sajbrfem. Viewed 11 November 2012. http://www.slideshare.net/sajbrfem/cyberfeminism-101.

Douglas, Danielle. 'Roots and Revenue: The Popularity of Natural Hairstyles is Lucrative for Local Salons.' The Washington Post, 7 March 2012. Viewed 21 March 2012. http://www.washingtonpost.com/business/capitalbusiness/roots-and-revenue-the-popularity-of-natural-hairstyles-is-lucrative-for-local-salons/2012/03/07/gIQAOkgL5R_story.html.

Fox, Mary Frank, Deborah G. Johnson, and Sue V. Rosser. Women, Gender and Technology. Champaign-Urbana: University of Illinois Press, 2006.

Hales, Kayla D. and Lynette Kvasny. 'Identity (Re)evaluation in Cyberspace' (paper presented at the International Conference on ICT for Africa 2010, Yaoundé, Cameroon, March 25-28, 2010. Viewed 28 July 2012.

http://faculty.ist.psu.edu/lkvasny/KvasnyHales-DigitalDivideChapter_Revised_.pdf.

Hesse-Biber, Sharlene Nagy, Stephanie A. Howling, Patricia Leavy, and Meg Lovejoy. 'Racial Identity and the Development of Body Image Issues among African American Adolescent Girls.' The Qualitative Report 9, no. 1 (March 2004): 67-69.

Hine, Christine. Virtual Ethnography. London: Sage Publications, 2000.

hooks, bell. Outlaw Culture: Resisting Representations. New York: Routledge, 1994.

Jacobs-Huey, Lanita. From the Kitchen to the Parlor: Language and African American Women's Hair Care. Oxford: Oxford University Press, 2006.

Kozinets, Robert V. Netnography: Doing Ethnographic Research Online. London: Sage Publications, 2010.

Macri, Gloria. 'Logging into Diaspora: Media and Online Identity Narratives amongst Romanians in Ireland.' Observatorio Journal 5, no. 2 (2011): 41-52.

Mercer, Kobena. Welcome to the Jungle. New York: Routledge, 1994.

Mintel Report Database MRd 2011, 'Black Hair Care -United States-August 2011.' Mintel.com. Viewed on 20 March 2012, http://www.oyxgen.mintel.com, 12.

Mitra, Ananda and Eric Watts, 'Theorizing Cyberspace: the Idea of Voice Applied to the Internet Discourse.' New Media and Society 4, no. 4 (2002): 479-498.

Nayer, Praymond K. An Introduction to New Media and Cybercultures. West Sussex: Wiley-Blackwell, 2010.

Nimrod, Galit. 'Online Communities as a Resource in Older Adults' Tourism.' The Journal of Community Informatics 8, no. 1 (2012): 4.

Preece, Jennifer and Dana Rotman. 'The "WeTube" in YouTube: Creating an Online Community through Video Sharing.' International Journal of Web Based Communities 6, no. 3 (2010): 317-333.

Qian, Yuxia and Yuping Mao. 'A Content Analysis of Online Social Support Behaviors of Overseas Chinese   Prenatal and Postnatal Women.' China Media Report Overseas, 2010. Viewed 21 May 2012. http://www.thefreelibrary.com/A+content+analysis+of+online+soci al+support+behaviors+of+overseas...-a0242509930.

Robinson, Cynthia. 'Hair as Race: Why 'Good Hair' May be Bad for Black Women.' Howard Journal of Communications 22, no.4 (2011): 358-376.

Rooks, Noliwe M. Hair Raising: Beauty, Culture and African

American Women. London and New Brunswick: Rutgers University Press, 1996.

Sade-Beck, Liav. 'Internet Ethnography: Online and Offline.' International Journal of Qualitative Methods 3, no. 2 (2004): 46-47.

Saro-Wiwa, Nina. 'Black Women's Transition to Natural Hair.' The New York Times. 1 June 2012. Viewed 11 June 2012. http://www.nytimes.com/2012/06/01/opinion/Black-women-and-natural-hair.html?_r=0.

Scruggs, Tricia. 'I Am Not My Hair: How YouTube Culture Powers Change.' viralmedia.pbworks.com Viewed on 13 November 2012. http://viralmedia.pbworks.com/w/file/fetch/53605654/I%20Am%20 Not%20My%20Hair-%20EMAC%206372.pdf.

Senft, Theresa M. Camgirls: Celebrity & Community in the Age of Social Networks. New York: Peter Lang Publishing, 2008.

Smith, Mark A. and Peter Kollock, eds. Communities in Cyberspace. London: Routledge, 1999.

Snickars, Pelle and Patrick Vondreau. The YouTube Reader. Stockholm: National Library of Sweden, 2009.

Strangelove, Michael. Watching YouTube: Extraordinary Videos by Ordinary People. Toronto: University of Toronto Press, 2010.

Swain, Fiana O. Negotiating Beauty Ideals: Perceptions of Beauty among Black Female University Students. MA thesis. Georgia State University, 2012.

Van Beneden, Peter. 'Viewer "Identification" with Characters on Television and Film Fiction.' Aber.ac.uk. 1998. Viewed on 22 May 2012, http://www.aber.ac.uk/media/Students/pjv9801.html.

Walker, Susannah. Style and Status: Selling Beauty to African American Women 1920-1975. Lexington: University of Kentucky Press, 2007.

White, Michele. 'Too Close To See: Men, Women, and Webcams.' New Media & Society 5, no. 1 (2003): 11.

Wilding, Faith. 'Where is the Feminism in Cyber Feminism?' N.paradoxa International Feminist Art Journal 2 (1998), ktpress.co.uk. Viewed 1 November 2012, http://www.ktpress.co.uk/pdf/vol2_npara_6_13_Wilding.pdf.

Wright, Michelle. 'Finding a Place in Cyberspace: Black Women, Technology, and Identity.' Frontiers: A Journal of Women Studies 26, no. 1 (2005): 48-59.

http://www.youtube.com.